SITTING

The guitar should rest comfortably on your lap. The right leg may be crossed over the left leg for added support.

STANDING

A guitar strap is used to hold the guitar in correct playing position. A strap may also be used in the sitting position.

CLASSICAL POSITION

The left leg is raised by a footstand, which places the guitar in a very secure position.

THE LEFT HAND

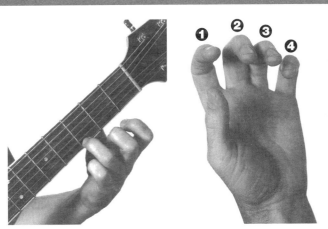

- The left-hand fingers are numbered 1, 2, 3, and 4 as shown.

- Press with the fingertip directly behind the fret. Use just enough pressure to produce a clear sound. For best results, the left-hand fingernails should be kept short.

- The thumb should touch lightly on the back of the guitar neck opposite the finger tips. It remains in a natural position. The palm does not touch the back of the neck.

THE RIGHT HAND

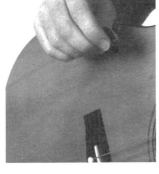

- The pick (flat-pick or plectrum) is used to strum the strings.

- Some students may choose to use the right-hand thumb and fingers instead of a pick.

- If using a **pick**, start with a teardrop shape of medium thickness.

- Hold the pick in a relaxed, secure way.

- The strings may be sounded by using **downstrokes** (⊓) or **upstrokes** (∨) with the guitar pick.

THE GUITAR FINGERBOARD

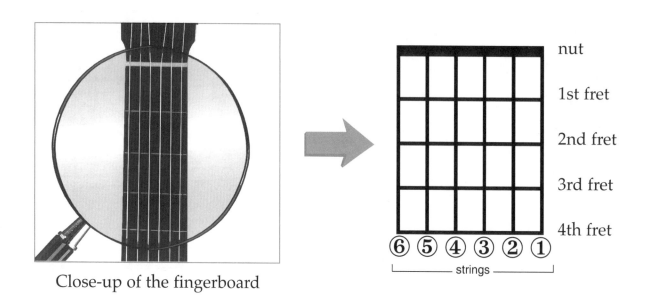

Close-up of the fingerboard

nut
1st fret
2nd fret
3rd fret
4th fret

⑥ ⑤ ④ ③ ② ①

strings

The guitar fingerboard shows you where to play each note.

- Dots (❶❷❸❹) show you where to place your left-hand fingers.
- A circle (○) indicates an open string; no left-hand fingers are used.
- An ✕ indicates strings that are not to be strummed.
- An ⊗ indicates strings that are strummed but **dampened**.
- A barre (⌢) indicates that one finger plays more than one string.
- The letters below the fingerboard indicate the names of the notes that are being played.

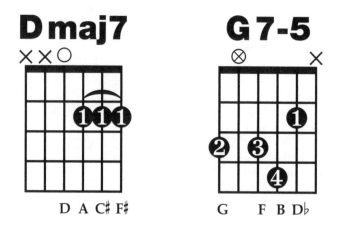

G1029

TUNING THE GUITAR

It is very important that your guitar be tuned correctly each time you practice.

1. Electronic tuner

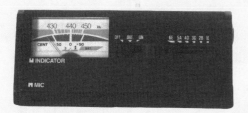

The *easiest* way to tune your guitar is with an electronic tuner, which comes with simple instructions. Electronic tuners are inexpensive and are used by many professional guitarists as well as beginning students.

2. Piano keyboard

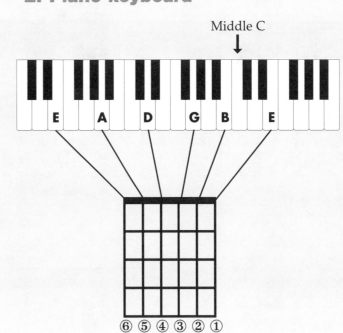

Your guitar can be tuned to a piano, an organ, or an electronic keyboard. Important: Notice the location of Middle C on the chart above.

3. Tuning the guitar to itself (relative tuning)

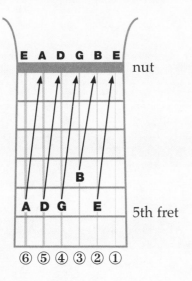

Assuming that string ⑥ is correctly tuned to **E**:			
PRESS	**STRING**	**TO GET THE PITCH**	**TO TUNE OPEN STRING**
the 5th fret of	⑥	**A**	⑤
the 5th fret of	⑤	**D**	④
the 5th fret of	④	**G**	③
the 4th fret of	③	**B**	②
the 5th fret of	②	**E**	①

MAJOR CHORDS

C

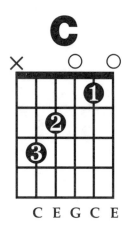

C E G C E

D

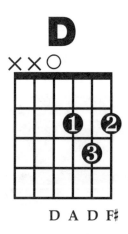

D A D F#

E

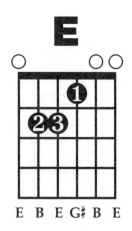

E B E G# B E

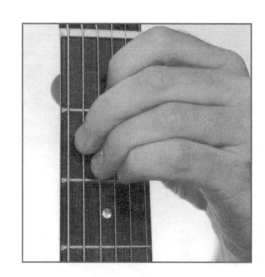

G1029

F

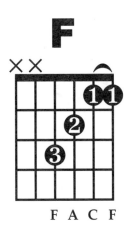

F A C F

G

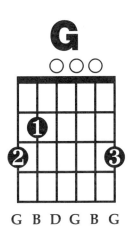

G B D G B G

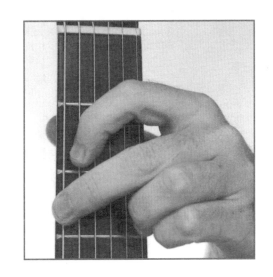

A

A E A C♯ E

MAJOR CHORDS

B

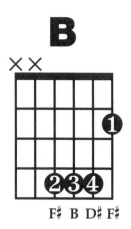

× ×

① ② ③ ④

F♯ B D♯ F♯

*B♭

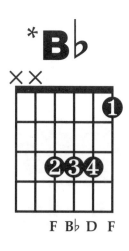

× ×

① ② ③ ④

F B♭ D F

D♭

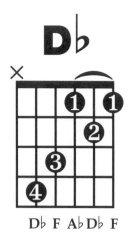

×

① ① ② ③ ④

D♭ F A♭ D♭ F

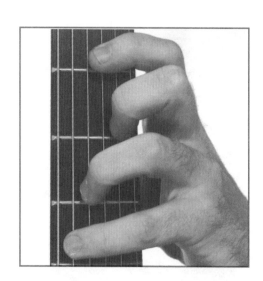

*Every flat chord has a sharp equivalent, and every sharp chord has a flat equivalent. See the term **enharmonic** in the Fact Finder on page 2.

G1029

MAJOR CHORDS

E♭

3fr.

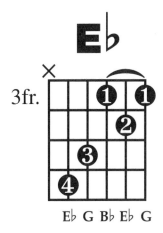

E♭ G B♭ E♭ G

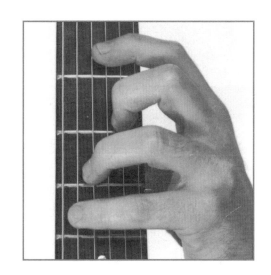

F♯

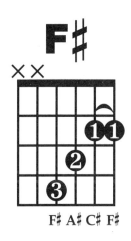

F♯ A♯ C♯ F♯

A♭

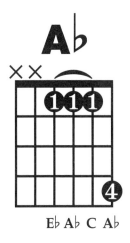

E♭ A♭ C A♭

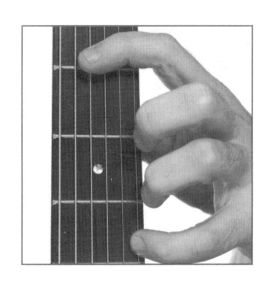

MINOR CHORDS

Cm

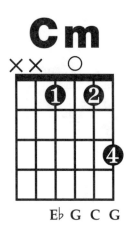

×× ○

① ②

④

E♭ G C G

Dm

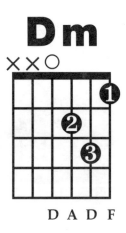

×× ○

①

②

③

D A D F

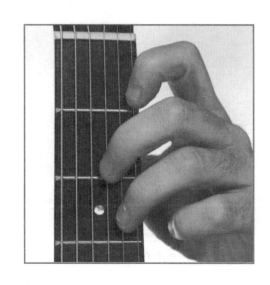

Em

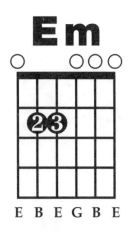

○ ○○○

②③

E B E G B E

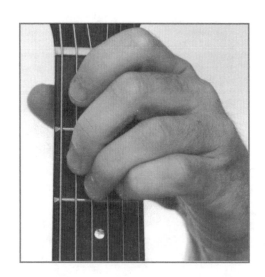

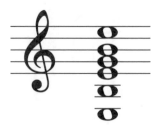

G1029

Fm

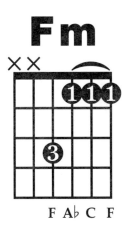

F A♭ C F

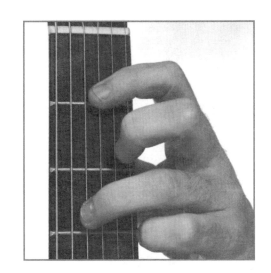

Gm

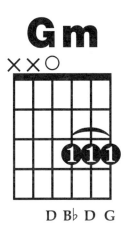

D B♭ D G

Am

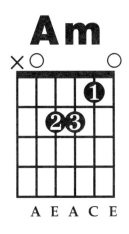

A E A C E

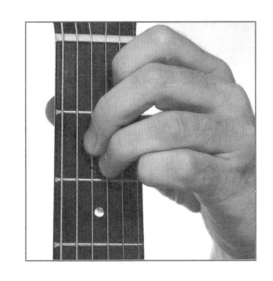

MINOR CHORDS

Bm
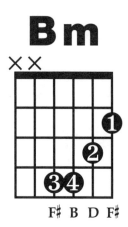

F# B D F#

B♭m
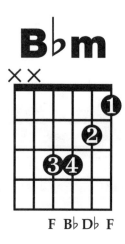

F B♭ D♭ F

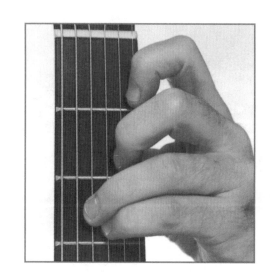

D♭m
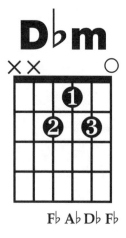

F♭ A♭ D♭ F♭

G1029

E♭m

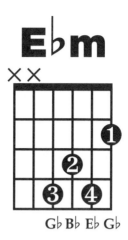

G♭ B♭ E♭ G♭

F♯m

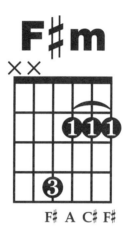

F♯ A C♯ F♯

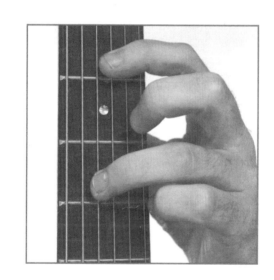

A♭m

4fr.

A♭ C♭ E♭ A♭

SEVENTH CHORDS

C7

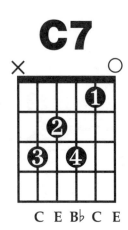

C E B♭ C E

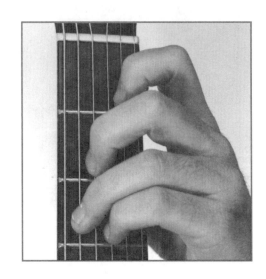

D7

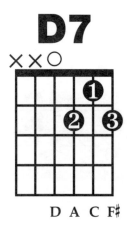

D A C F♯

E7

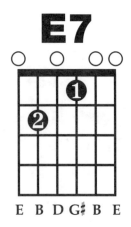

E B D G♯ B E

F7

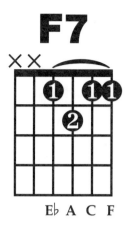

Eb A C F

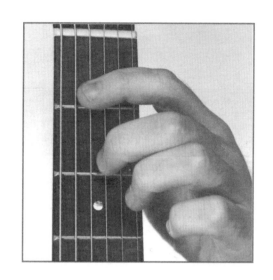

G7

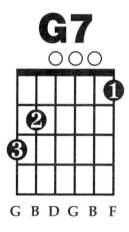

G B D G B F

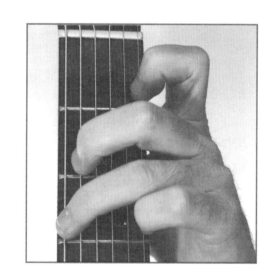

A7

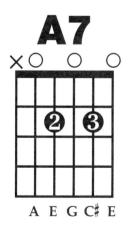

A E G C# E

SEVENTH CHORDS

B7

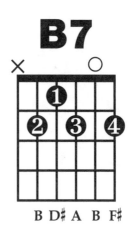

B D# A B F#

B♭7

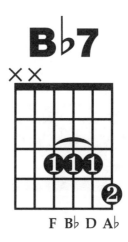

F B♭ D A♭

D♭7

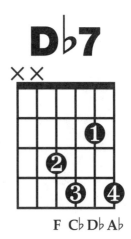

F C♭ D♭ A♭

G1029

E♭7

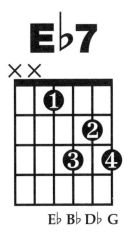

× ×

①
②
③ ④

E♭ B♭ D♭ G

F#7

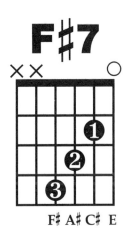

× × ○

①
②
③

F# A# C# E

A♭7

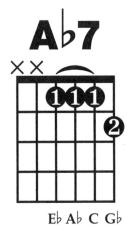

× ×

① ① ①
②

E♭ A♭ C G♭

MINOR SEVENTH CHORDS

Cm7

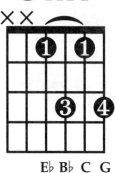

Eb Bb C G

Dm7

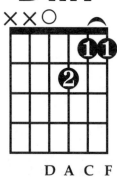

D A C F

Em7

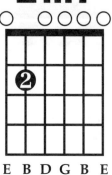

E B D G B E

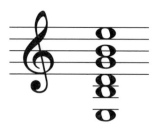

Fm7

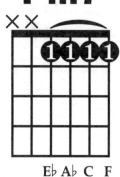

Eb Ab C F

G1029

MINOR SEVENTH CHORDS

Gm7

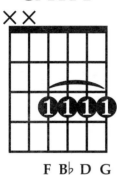

F Bb D G

Am7

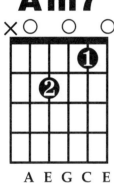

A E G C E

Bm7

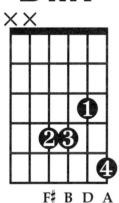

F# B D A

Bbm7

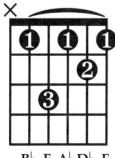

Bb F Ab Db F

MINOR SEVENTH CHORDS

D♭m7

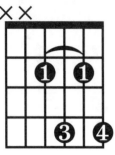

F♭ C♭ D♭ A♭

E♭m7

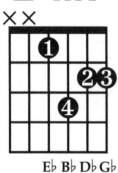

E♭ B♭ D♭ G♭

F#m7

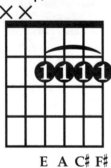

E A C# F#

A♭m7

G♭ C♭ E♭ A♭

G1029

Cmaj7

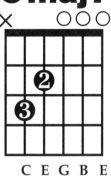

C E G B E

Dmaj7

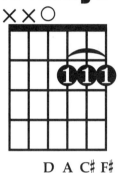

D A C# F#

Emaj7

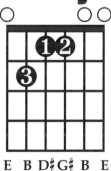

E B D# G# B E

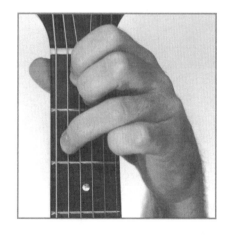

Fmaj7

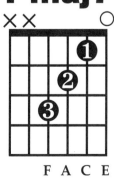

F A C E

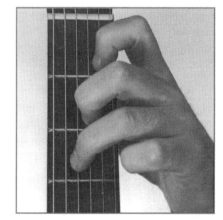

G1029

MAJOR SEVENTH CHORDS

Gmaj7

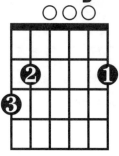

G B D G B F#

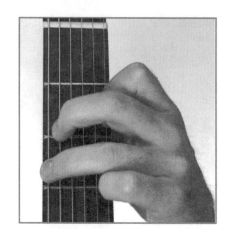

Amaj7

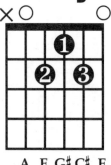

A E G# C# E

Bmaj7

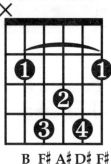

B F# A# D# F#

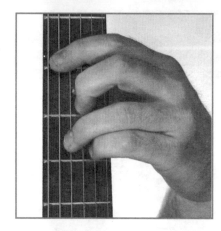

B♭maj7

B♭ F A D F

G1029

D♭maj7

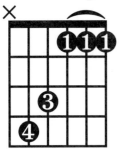

D♭ F A♭ C F

E♭maj7

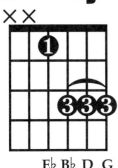

E♭ B♭ D G

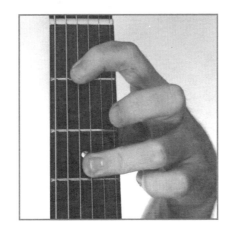

F#maj7

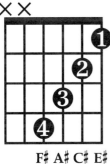

F# A# C# E#

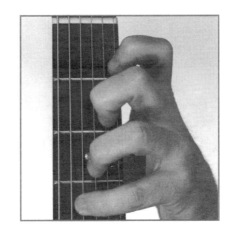

A♭maj7

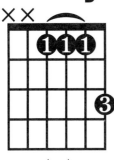

E♭ A♭ C G

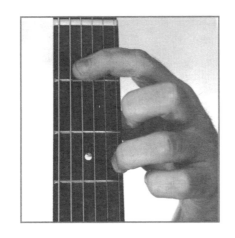

G1029

POWER CHORDS

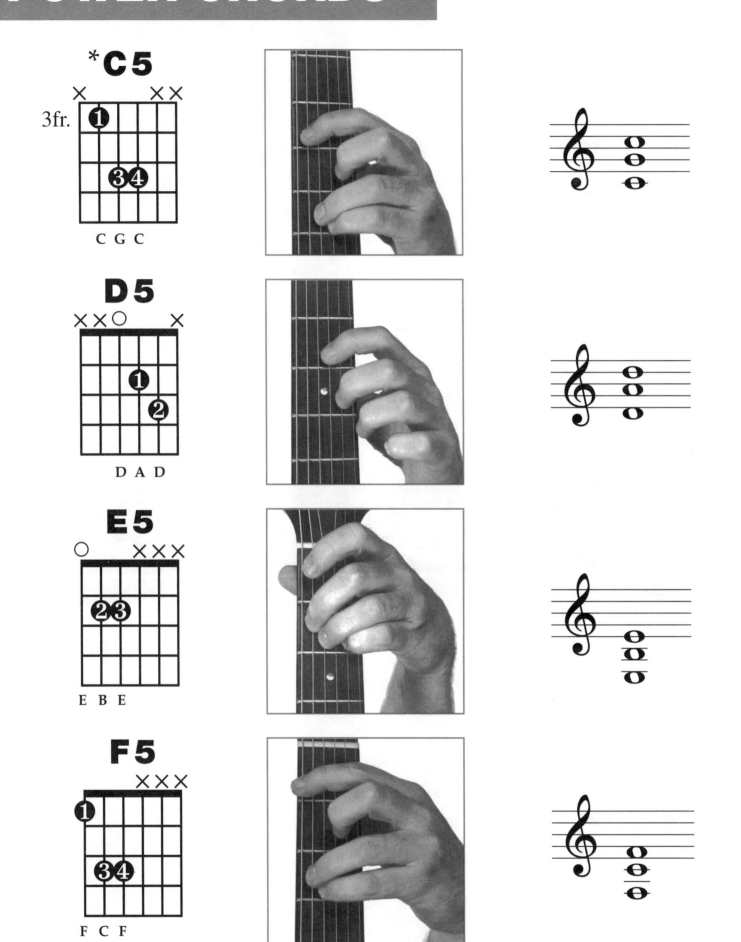

*C5

3fr.

C G C

D5

D A D

E5

E B E

F5

F C F

* The highest-pitched note in a **Power Chord** may be omitted.

24

G1029

G 5

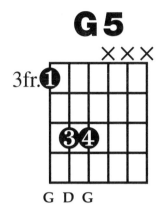

3fr.

G D G

A 5

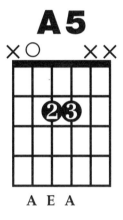

A E A

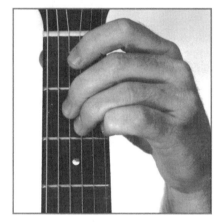

B 5

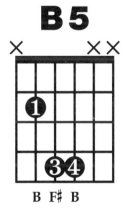

B F♯ B

B♭ 5

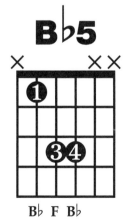

B♭ F B♭

G1029

POWER CHORDS

D♭5

4fr.

× × ×

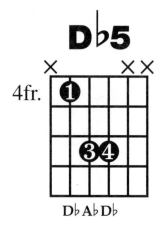

D♭ A♭ D♭

E♭5

× × ×

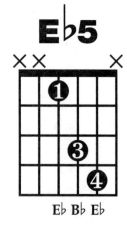

E♭ B♭ E♭

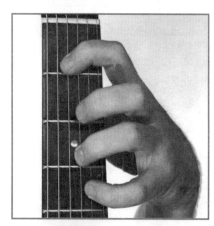

F♯5

× × ×

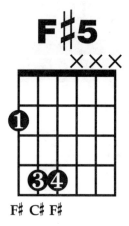

F♯ C♯ F♯

A♭5

4fr.

× × ×

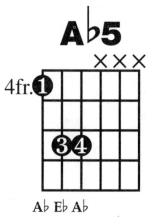

A♭ E♭ A♭

G1029

C 6

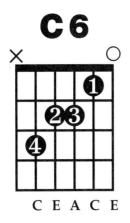

C E A C E

D 6

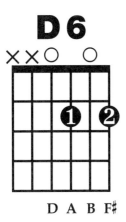

D A B F#

E 6

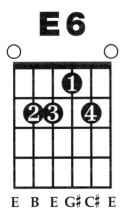

E B E G# C# E

F 6

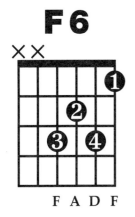

F A D F

SIXTH CHORDS

G 6

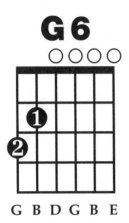

G B D G B E

A 6

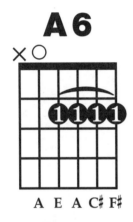

A E A C# F#

B 6

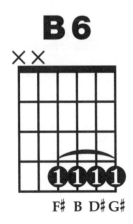

F# B D# G#

B♭6

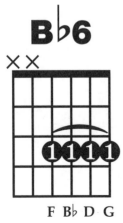

F B♭ D G

G1029

D♭6

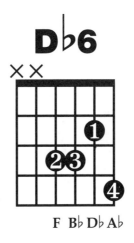

F B♭ D♭ A♭

E♭6

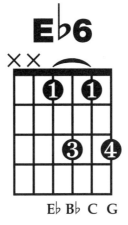

E♭ B♭ C G

F♯6

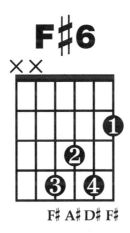

F♯ A♯ D♯ F♯

A♭6

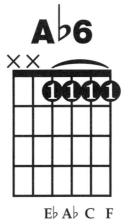

E♭ A♭ C F

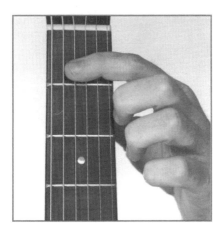

G1029

MINOR SIXTH CHORDS

Cm6

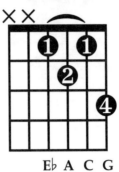

×× 1 1 2 4

Eb A C G

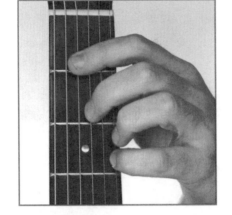

Dm6

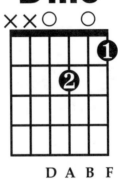

×× ○ ○ 2 1

D A B F

Em6

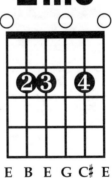

○ ○ ○ 2 3 4

E B E G C# E

Fm6

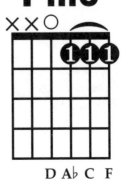

×× ○ 1 1 1

D Ab C F

G1029

MINOR SIXTH CHORDS

Gm6

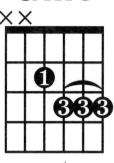

E B♭ D G

Am6

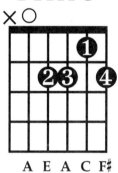

A E A C F#

Bm6

D G# B F#

B♭m6

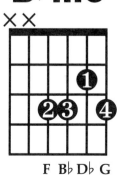

F B♭ D♭ G

G1029

31

MINOR SIXTH CHORDS

D♭m6

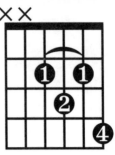

F♭ B♭ D♭ A♭

E♭m6

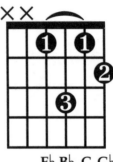

E♭ B♭ C G♭

F♯m6

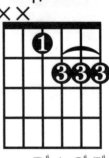

D♯ A C♯ F♯

A♭m6

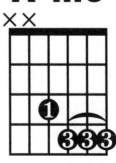

F C♭ E♭ A♭

G1029

C9

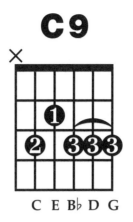

C E B♭ D G

D9

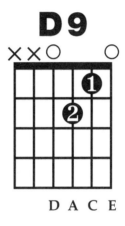

D A C E

E9

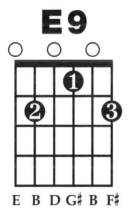

E B D G♯ B F♯

F9

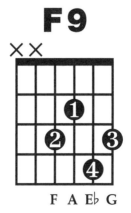

F A E♭ G

NINTH CHORDS

G9

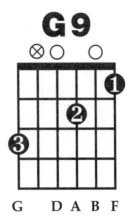

G D A B F

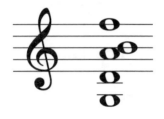

A9

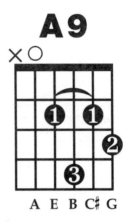

A E B C# G

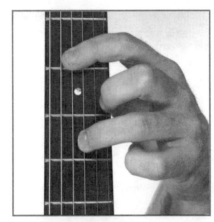

B9

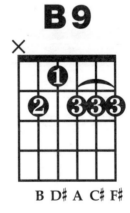

B D# A C# F#

B♭9

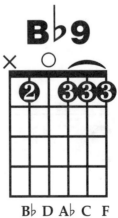

B♭ D A♭ C F

34

G1029

D♭9

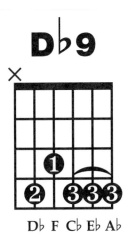

Db F Cb Eb Ab

E♭9

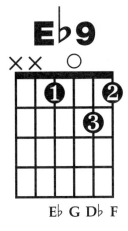

Eb G Db F

F#9

3fr.

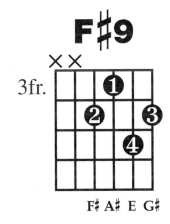

F# A# E G#

A♭9

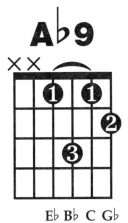

Eb Bb C Gb

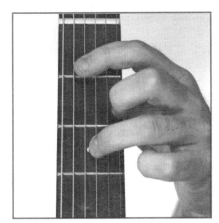

SUSPENDED FOURTH CHORDS

C sus4

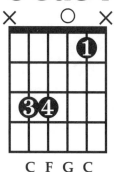

C F G C

D sus4

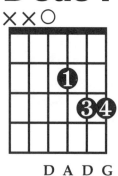

D A D G

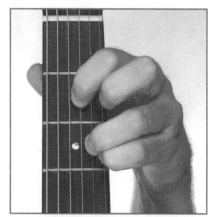

E sus4

E B E A B E

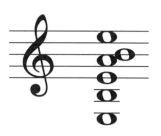

F sus4

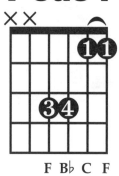

F B♭ C F

G sus4

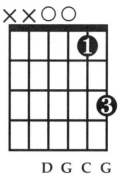

D G C G

A sus4

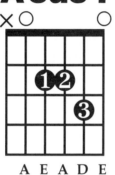

A E A D E

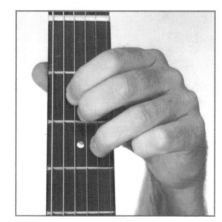

B sus4

2fr.

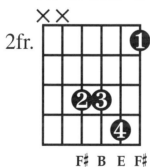

F# B E F#

Bb sus4

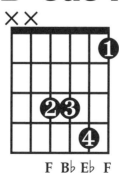

F Bb Eb F

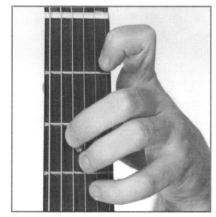

D♭sus4

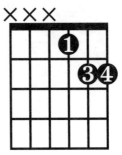

A♭ D♭ G♭

E♭sus4

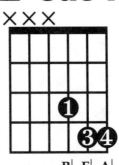

B♭ E♭ A♭

F♯sus4

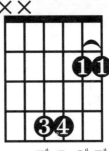

F♯ B C♯ F♯

A♭sus4

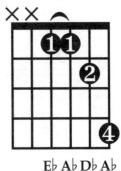

E♭ A♭ D♭ A♭

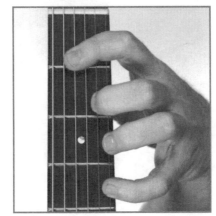

G1029

7+5 CHORDS

C 7+5

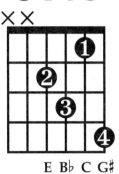
E B♭ C G#
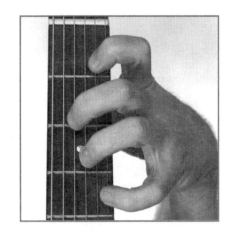

D 7+5
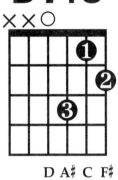
D A# C F#

E 7+5
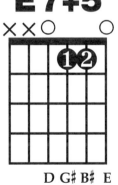
D G# B# E

F 7+5
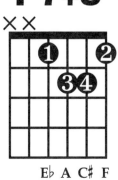
E♭ A C# F

7+5 CHORDS

G 7+5

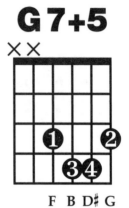

F B D♯ G

A 7+5

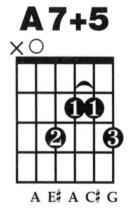

A E♯ A C♯ G

B 7+5

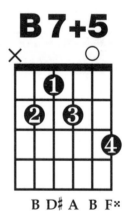

B D♯ A B F✕

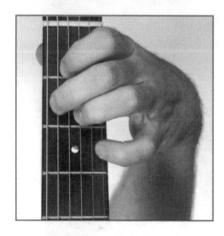

B♭7+5

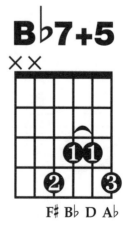

F♯ B♭ D A♭

G1029

7+5 CHORDS

D♭7+5

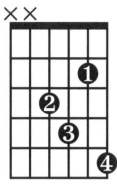

F C♭ D♭ A

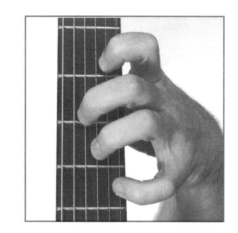

E♭7+5

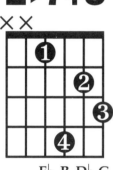

E♭ B D♭ G

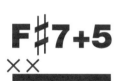

F♯7+5

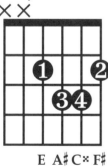

E A♯ C× F♯

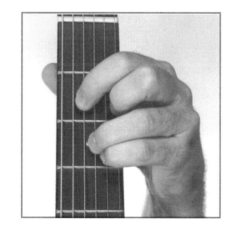

A♭7+5

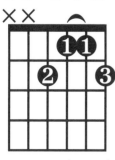

E A♭ C G♭

G1029

41

C 7-5

3fr.

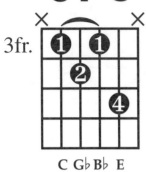

C G♭ B♭ E

D 7-5

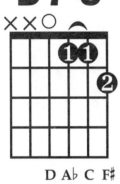

D A♭ C F#

E 7-5

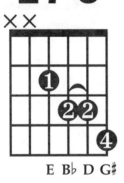

E B♭ D G#

F 7-5

3fr.

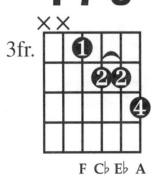

F C♭ E♭ A

G 7-5

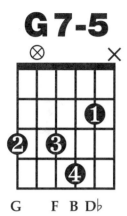

G F B D♭

A 7-5

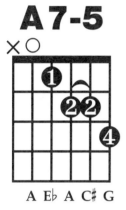

A E♭ A C♯ G

B 7-5

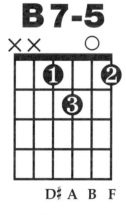

D♯ A B F

B♭ 7-5

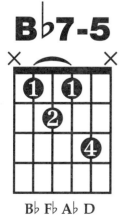

B♭ F♭ A♭ D

7-5 CHORDS

D♭7-5

× ×

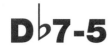

F C♭ D♭ A♭♭

E♭7-5

× ×

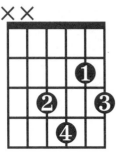

E♭ B♭♭ D♭ G

F♯7-5

× ×

4fr.

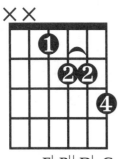

F♯ C E A♯

A♭7-5

× × ○

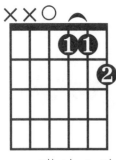

E♭♭ A♭ C G♭

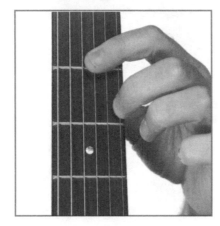

G1029

DIMINISHED SEVENTH CHORDS

A **diminished seventh chord** (dim7, °7) may be named after any one of its chord tones. For example, Fdim7 may also be named Ddim7, A♭dim7 (G♯dim7), or Bdim7. Every note may be considered a root.

Fdim7

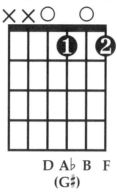

× × ○ ○

D A♭ B F
(G♯)

F♯dim7

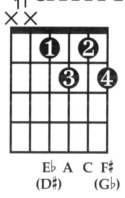

× ×

E♭ A C F♯
(D♯)   (G♭)

Gdim7

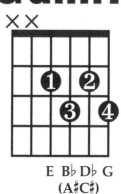

× ×

E B♭ D♭ G
(A♯C♯)

AUGMENTED CHORDS

An **augmented chord** (+, +5, aug, #5) may be named after any one of its chord tones. For example, E+ may also be named G#+ (Ab+) or C+. Every note may be considered a root.

E+

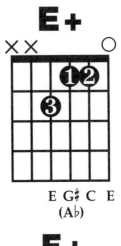

E G# C E
(Ab)

F+

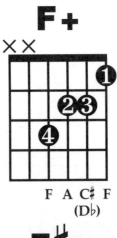

F A C# F
(Db)

F#+

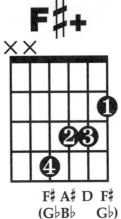

F# A# D F#
(GbBb   Gb)

G+

G B D# G
(Eb)

G1029

MOVABLE CHORDS

Chords that use no open strings have a special feature. They may be moved up and down the fingerboard to form other chords. There are three common movable chord families on the guitar. The E, A, and C types of **movable chords** use the same *shapes* as the basic chords they are named after. By adding a *barre* (using one left-hand finger to play more than one string at a time), you can move the same shape up and down the fingerboard to make different chords.

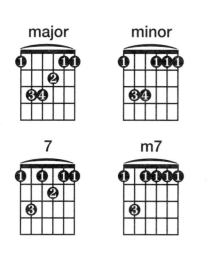

E-TYPE MOVABLE CHORDS

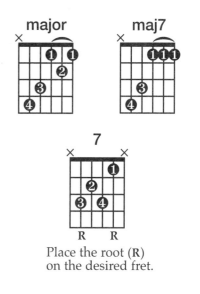

A-TYPE MOVABLE CHORDS

C-TYPE MOVABLE CHORDS

Place the root (R) on the desired fret.

FIRST FINGER BARRE	E TYPE	A TYPE	C TYPE
Open (no barre)	E	A	C
1st Fret	F	A♯ (or B♭)	C♯ (or D♭)
2nd Fret	F♯ (or G♭)	B	D
3rd Fret	G	C	D♯ (or E♭)
4th Fret	G♯ (or A♭)	C♯ (or D♭)	E
5th Fret	A	D	F
6th Fret	A♯ (or B♭)	D♯ (or E♭)	F♯ (or G♭)
7th Fret	B	E	G
8th Fret	C	F	G♯ (or A♭)
9th Fret	C♯ (or D♭)	F♯ (or G♭)	A
10th Fret	D	G	A♯ (or B♭)
11th Fret	D♯ (or E♭)	G♯ (or A♭)	B
12th Fret	E	A	C
13th Fret	F	A♯ (or B♭)	C♯ (or D♭)

USING A CAPO

A **capo** is a clamp that holds all six strings down on any given fret, raising the pitch of the open strings by one half step for every fret. For example, a capo placed on the first fret will make an E chord sound like an F, an A chord sound like a B♭, etc.

Using a Capo To Simplify a Difficult Key

A capo allows you to play comfortably in any key. For example, a song may be too hard to play in the key of E♭. One solution is to attach a capo on the third fret and play it as if it were in the key of C. You will, however, have to **transpose** every chord. Write the capoed chord name above the original chord. Your teacher will help you.

Using a Capo To Play in Different Keys

A capo may be used to change the key of a song for a more comfortable singing range. The following chart will help you play in common guitar keys while the guitar *sounds* in another:

CAPO THIS FRET ↓	PLAY IN THESE "GUITAR" KEYS				
	A	C	D	E	G
	CAPOED GUITAR SOUNDS IN THESE KEYS				
1	B♭ (or A♯)	D♭ (or C♯)	E♭ (or D♯)	F	A♭ (or G♯)
2	B	D	E	G♭ (or F♯)	A
3	C	E♭ (or D♯)	F	G	B♭ (or A♯)
4	D♭ (or C♯)	E	G♭ (or F♯)	A♭ (or G♯)	B
5	D	F	G	A	C
6	E♭ (or D♯)	G♭ (or F♯)	A♭ (or G♯)	B♭ (or A♯)	D♭ (or C♯)
7	E	G	A	B	D
8	F	A♭ (or G♯)	B♭ (or A♯)	C	E♭ (or D♯)
9	G♭ (or F♯)	A	B	D♭ (or C♯)	E
10	G	B♭ (or A♯)	C	D	F
11	A♭ (or G♯)	B	D♭ (or C♯)	E♭ (or D♯)	G♭ (or F♯)

G1029